CAVES

Deep in the earth there are dark, mysterious caves.
Some are tiny—just the right size for a mother fox and
her little ones. Others are huge—bigger than a tall
building. Strange fish live in some of these vast caverns,
and icicles of stone hang from their ceilings. In rocky
cliffs along the ocean shore, pirates long ago found
caves where they could hide their treasure. No one knows
how many caves there are in the whole world, but
"spelunkers" are always finding new ones to explore.

Roma Gans describes the many kinds of caves and
explains how they are formed. Drawing on her own
experience of caves around the country, she gives an
enticing view of this underground world.

CAVES

BY ROMA GANS

ILLUSTRATED BY
GIULIO MAESTRO

THOMAS Y. CROWELL COMPANY · NEW YORK

LET'S-READ-AND-FIND-OUT SCIENCE BOOKS

Editors: *DR. ROMA GANS*, Professor Emeritus of Childhood Education, Teachers College, Columbia University
DR. FRANKLYN M. BRANLEY, Astronomer Emeritus and former Chairman of The American Museum–Hayden Planetarium

AIR, WATER, AND WEATHER

Air Is All Around You
The Clean Brook
Flash, Crash, Rumble, and Roll
Floating and Sinking
Icebergs
North, South, East, and West
Oxygen Keeps You Alive
Rain and Hail
Snow Is Falling
Sunshine Makes the Seasons
Water for Dinosaurs and You
Where the Brook Begins

THE EARTH AND ITS COMPOSITION

The Bottom of the Sea
Caves

Fossils Tell of Long Ago
Glaciers
A Map Is a Picture
Millions and Millions of Crystals
Oil: The Buried Treasure
Salt
Where Does the Garbage Go?
The Wonder of Stones

ASTRONOMY AND SPACE

The Beginning of the Earth
The Big Dipper
Eclipse: Darkness in Daytime
The Moon Seems to Change
Rockets and Satellites
The Sun: Our Nearest Star
What Makes Day and Night
*What the Moon Is Like**

MATTER AND ENERGY

Energy from the Sun
Gravity Is a Mystery
High Sounds, Low Sounds
Hot as an Ice Cube
Light and Darkness
The Listening Walk
Streamlined
Upstairs and Downstairs
Weight and Weightlessness
What Makes a Shadow?

And other books on LIVING THINGS: PLANTS; LIVING THINGS: ANIMALS, BIRDS, FISH, INSECTS, ETC.; and THE HUMAN BODY

* Available in Spanish.

Library of Congress Cataloging in Publication Data Gans, Roma, date. Caves. SUMMARY: A simple introduction to caves, their formation, past uses, and distinguishing features. 1. Caves—Juv. lit. [1. Caves] I. Maestro, Giulio. II. Title. GB601.2.G35 551.4'4 76-4881 ISBN 0-690-01070-2 (CQR)

1 2 3 4 5 6 7 8 9 10

CAVES

There are thousands and thousands of caves in the world. Nobody knows how many.

Some caves are small, just large enough to hide a mother fox and the young foxes. Some are very large and very deep. A tall building could be built in one of them. Your school and playground could fit into a large cave.

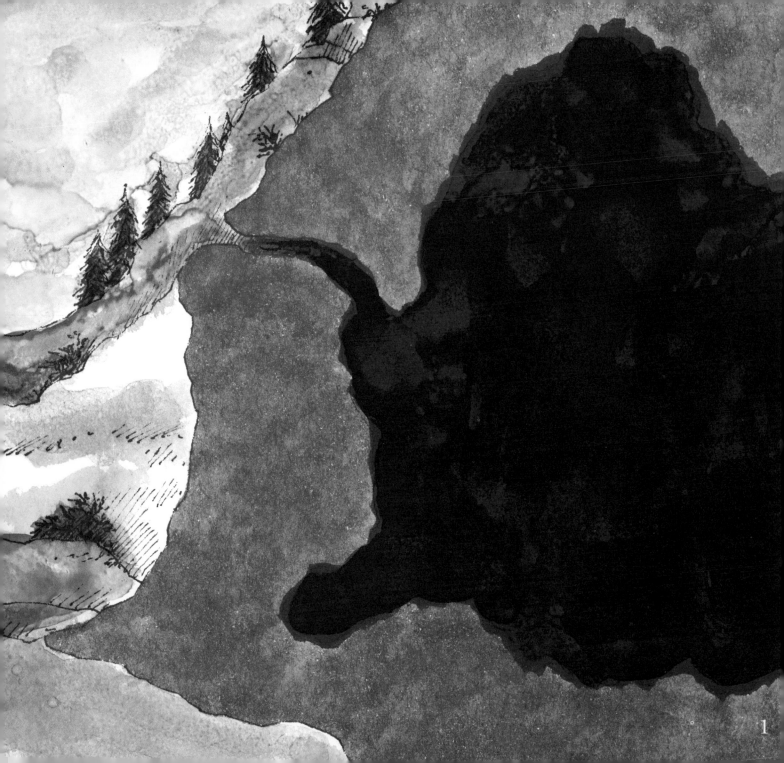

Some caves have low, narrow places between big, wide rooms. People must crawl through tunnels to go from one place to the next.

Most caves are damp. The floor may be wet and slippery. Water often drips from the walls and ceiling. The air smells moldy.

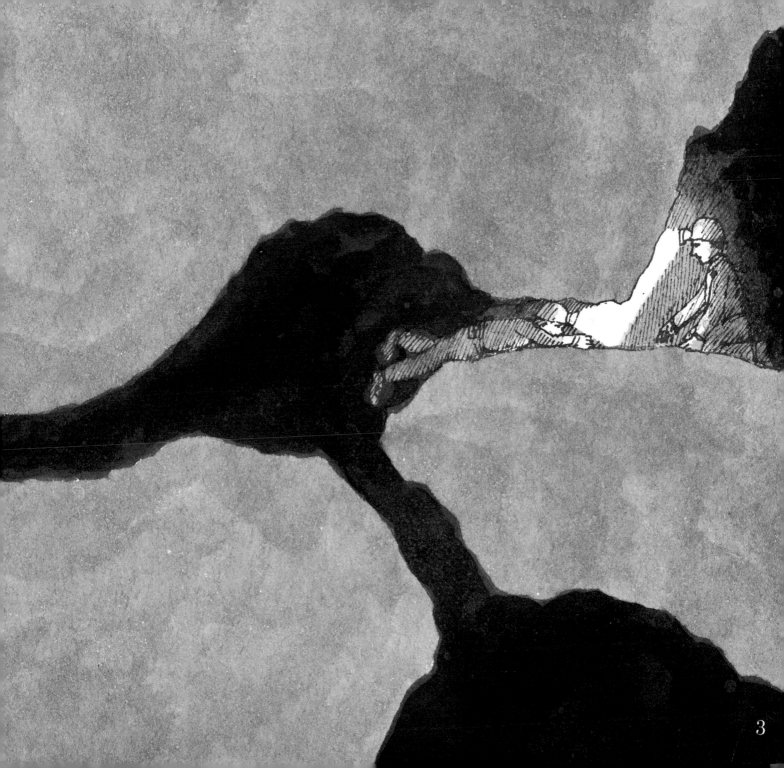

3

4

In some caves water trickles from place to place. There are underground pools and lakes. In some places there are deep streams. Sometimes the streams disappear. The water runs into openings in the floor. The river may come out in another part of the cave, or it may flow out of the cave into a valley.

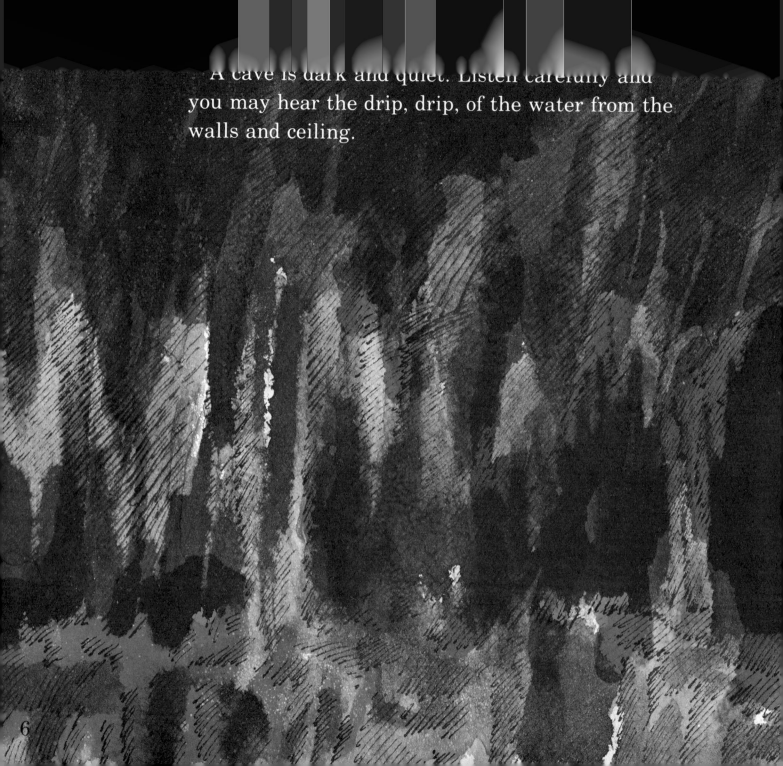

A cave is dark and quiet. Listen carefully and you may hear the drip, drip, of the water from the walls and ceiling.

Caves are darker than the darkest night. The
sun never shines in them. The moon and stars
don't, either. You need a flashlight to see. No trees
or grass or flowers can grow in caves because

Blind, white fish swim in some pools and lakes in caves.

Bats hang from the ceilings. They fly out at night to catch insects for their food.

In summer the air in caves is cooler than the air outside. But in winter it is warmer. The temperature in caves stays about the same all year round.

Hundreds of years ago in North America, Indians lived in caves. Some of their tools and pots have been found, and even ashes left from their fires.

Many thousands of years ago almost all people lived in caves. Their paintings on the walls tell us about them. Some of their tools and pots have also been found, and even some of their garbage.

Some caves can be very windy. One in South
Dakota is called the Wind Cave. First the winds
blow in one direction. Then in the other. People
light candles and watch the winds blow the flames.
Often the wind is so strong it puts out the candles.
Winds blow out of the cave when the air pressure
outside drops and the weather is turning rainy.
They blow into the cave when air pressure rises
and the weather is clearing up.

Most large caves are formed in a kind of rock
called limestone. Limestone can be washed away.

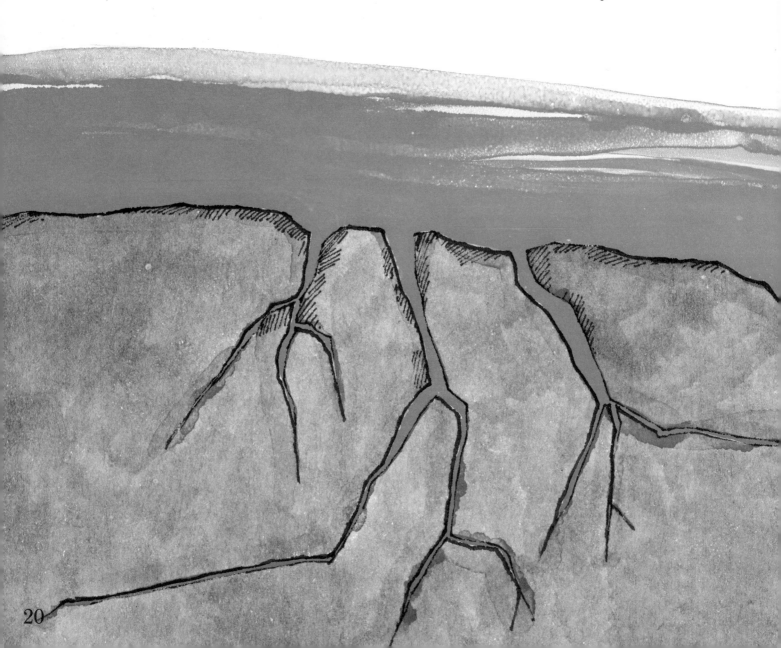

Water gets into cracks in the limestone. The water has carbon dioxide in it. It gets the carbon dioxide from the air. Water and carbon dioxide together make an acid. The acid slowly dissolves the limestone. The cracks grow larger and deeper.

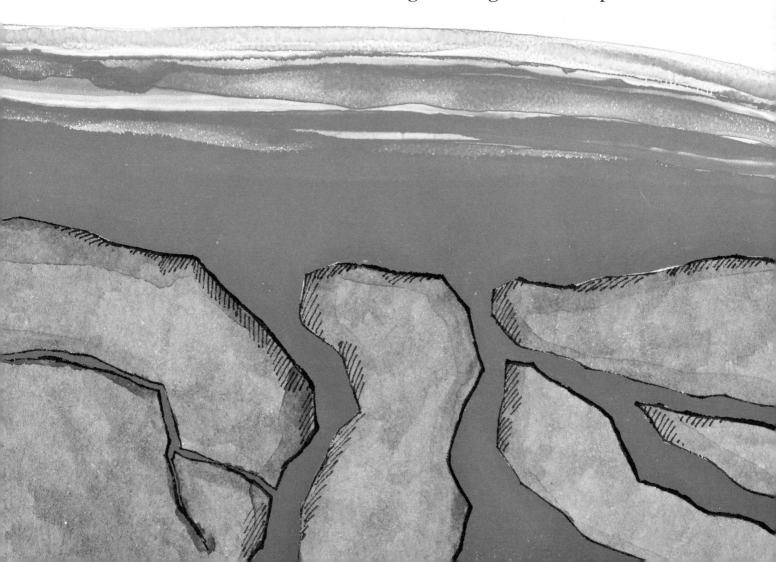

Most of the dissolved limestone is carried away by the water. After millions of years, the cracks in the limestone become big caves. A very large cave is called a cavern. Caverns have many large rooms that are connected by tunnels.

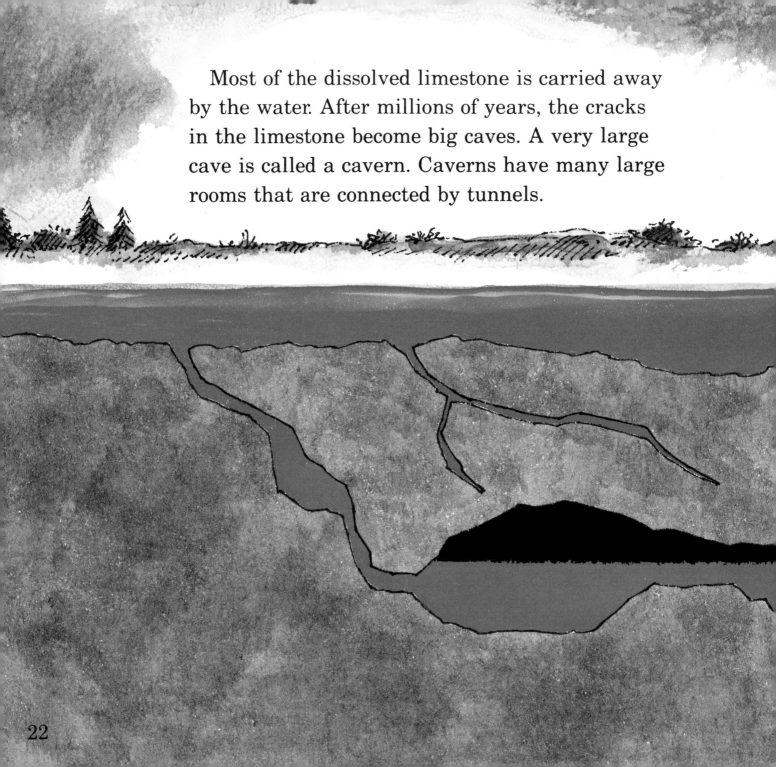

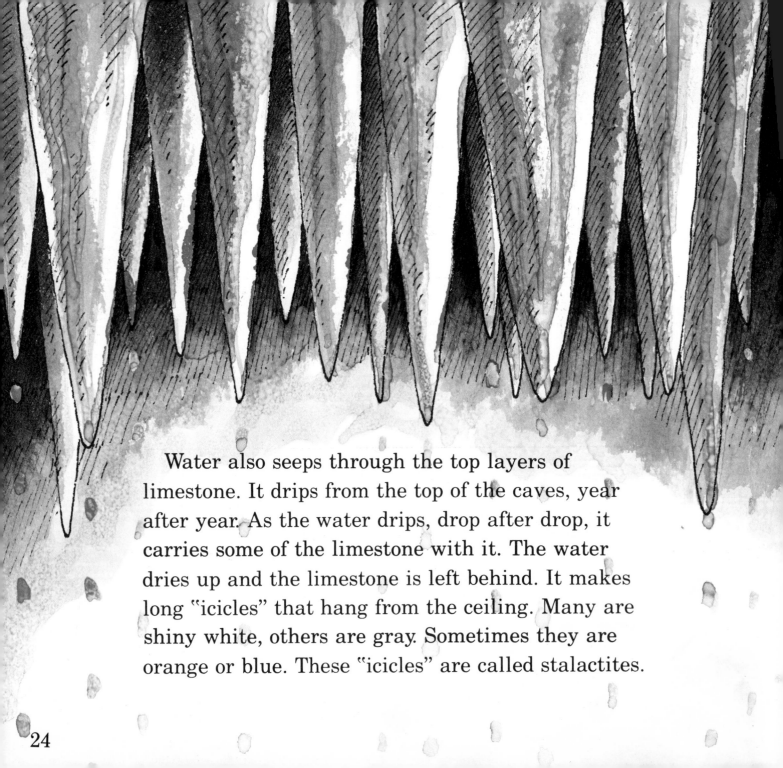

Water also seeps through the top layers of limestone. It drips from the top of the caves, year after year. As the water drips, drop after drop, it carries some of the limestone with it. The water dries up and the limestone is left behind. It makes long "icicles" that hang from the ceiling. Many are shiny white, others are gray. Sometimes they are orange or blue. These "icicles" are called stalactites.

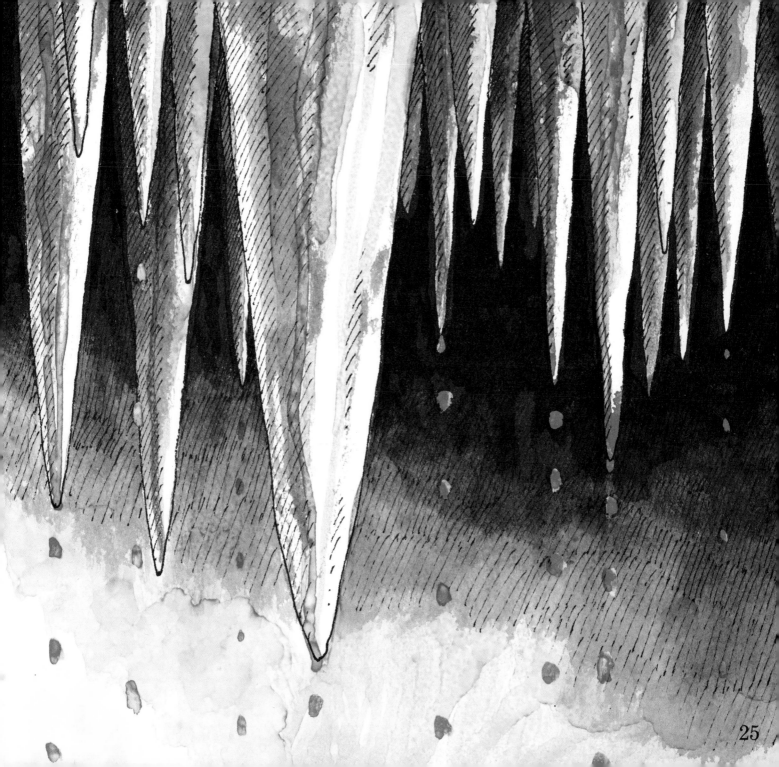

In many places the water drips, drop after drop, to the ground. After centuries, limestone mounds are made on the floor of the cave. They are called stalagmites. In some places a stalactite and a stalagmite meet and form a column of stone.

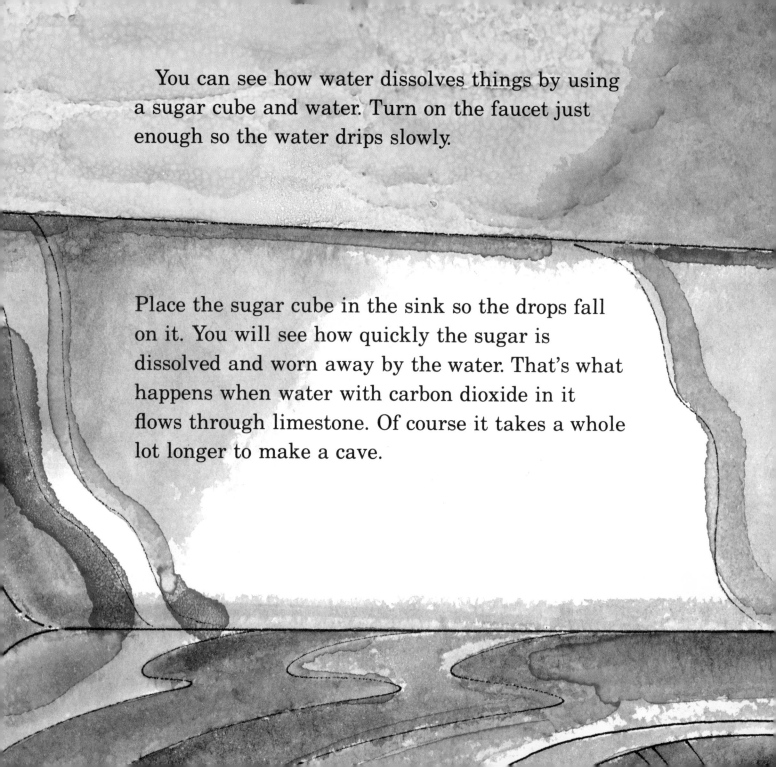

You can see how water dissolves things by using a sugar cube and water. Turn on the faucet just enough so the water drips slowly.

Place the sugar cube in the sink so the drops fall on it. You will see how quickly the sugar is dissolved and worn away by the water. That's what happens when water with carbon dioxide in it flows through limestone. Of course it takes a whole lot longer to make a cave.

Water also makes other kinds of caves. Along the ocean shores there are big caves. They were made by the waves of the ocean. The waves pounded against the shore, carrying sand and stones with them. A cave was left where the shore rock was worn away by the waves.

Pirates found these caves. They hid their stolen treasures in them. Some of these hidden treasures have never been found.

Someday you may explore a cave. If you do, be sure to go with an expert. Scientists who study caves are called speleologists. Other persons who are interested in exploring caves are called spelunkers. Spelunkers always take good flashlights with them. As they explore a cave they sometimes unwind rope. The rope helps them find their way back out of the cave.

Spelunkers and speleologists would rather explore a cave than go swimming or play baseball. They try to find out more about how caves were formed and how old they are.

Most of all, spelunkers want to find new caves to explore.

ABOUT THE AUTHOR

Roma Gans has called children "enlightened, excited citizens." She believes in the fundamental theory that children are eager to learn and will whet their own intellectual curiosity if they have stimulating teachers and books. She herself is the author of ten previous books in the Let's-Read-and-Find-Out series.

Dr. Gans received her B.S. from Columbia Teachers College and her Ph.D. from Columbia University. She began her work in the education field in the public schools of the Middle West as a teacher, supervisor, and assistant superintendent of schools. She is Professor Emeritus of Childhood Education at Teachers College, Columbia University, and lectures extensively throughout the United States and Canada.

Dr. Gans lives in West Redding, Connecticut, where she enjoys observing the many aspects of nature.

ABOUT THE ILLUSTRATOR

Giulio Maestro was born in New York City and studied at the Cooper Union Art School and the Pratt Graphics Center. He has illustrated many books for children, including several written by his wife, Betsy, a kindergarten teacher. In addition to his picture-book illustration, Mr. Maestro is well known for his beautiful hand lettering and his book jacket designs. He lives in Madison, Connecticut.